# What Product Managers Need To Know About World-Class Product Development

*How Product Managers Can Create Successful Products*

*"Practical, proven examples of how to work with development teams in order to have a successful product"*

## Dr. Jim Anderson

Published by:
Blue Elephant Consulting
Tampa, Florida

Copyright © 2013 by Dr. Jim Anderson

All rights reserved. No part of this book may be reproduced of transmitted in any form or by any means, electronic or mechanical, including photocopying, recording or by any information storage and retrieval system without written permission of the publisher, except for inclusion of brief quotations in a review.

Printed in the United States of America

Library of Congress Control Number: 2016952588

ISBN-13: 978-1537307985
ISBN-10: 1537307983

**Warning – Disclaimer**

The purpose of this book is to educate and entertain. This book does not promise or guarantee that anyone following the ideas, tips, suggestions, techniques or strategies will be successful. The author, publisher and distributor(s) shall have neither liability nor responsibility to anyone with respect to any loss or damage caused, or alleged to be caused, directly or indirectly by the information contained in this book.

# Recent Books By The Author

**Product Management**

- Customer Lessons For Product Managers: Techniques For Product Managers To Better Understand What Their Customers Really Want

- Product Failure Lessons For Product Managers: Examples Of Products That Have Failed For Product Managers To Learn From

**Public Speaking**

- How To Rehearse In Order To Give The Perfect Speech: How to effectively rehearse your next speech to that your message be remembered forever!

- Secrets To Creating The Perfect Speech: How to create a speech that will make your message be remembered forever!

**CIO Skills**

- How CIOs Can Make Innovation Happen: Tips And Techniques For CIOs To Use In Order To Make Innovation Happen In Their IT Department

- CIO Communication Skills Secrets: Tips And Techniques For CIOs To Use In Order To Become Better Communicators

**IT Manager Skills**

- Secrets Of Effective Leadership For IT Managers: Tips And Techniques That IT Managers Can Use In Order To Develop Leadership Skills

- IT Manager Career Secrets: Tips And Techniques That IT Managers Can Use In Order To Have A Successful Career

**Negotiating**

- Getting Ready To Win: How To Prepare For A Negotiation: What You Need To Do BEFORE A Negotiation Starts In Order To Get The Best Possible Deal

- Learn How To Argue In Your Next Negotiation: How To Develop The Skill Of Effective Arguing In A Negotiation In Order To Get The Best Possible Outcome

**Miscellaneous**

- Power Distribution Unit (PDU) Secrets: What Everyone Who Works In A Data Center Needs To Know!

- Making The Jump: How To Land Your Dream Job When You Get Out Of College!

**Note**: See a complete list of books by Dr. Jim Anderson at the back of this book.

# **Acknowledgements**

Any book like this one is the result of years of real-world work experience. In my over 25 years of working for 7 different firms, I have met countless fantastic people and I've been mentored by some truly exceptional ones. Although I've probably forgotten some of the people who made me the person that I am today, here is my attempt to finally give them the recognition that they so truly deserve:

- Thomas P. Anderson
- Art Puett
- Bobbi Marshall
- Bob Boggs

Dr. Jim Anderson

*This book is dedicated to my wife Lori. None of this would have been possible without her love and support.*

*Thanks for the best years of my life (so far)...!*

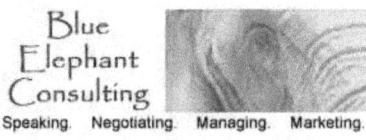

# Table Of Contents

IT'S ALL ABOUT THE PRODUCT ........................................................8

ABOUT THE AUTHOR ......................................................................10

CHAPTER 1: HOW CAN PRODUCT MANAGERS PICK THE RIGHT TECHNOLOGY FOR OUR PRODUCTS? ...............................................15

CHAPTER 2: PRODUCT MANAGERS NEED TO KNOW WHAT THEIR COMPANY'S COST OF CAPITAL IS......................................................18

CHAPTER 3: HOW PRODUCT MANAGERS CAN MANAGE THE AGE GAP ON THEIR PRODUCT TEAMS ...........................................................24

CHAPTER 4: HOW YAHOO PRODUCT MANAGERS ARE KICKING GOOGLE'S BUTT ............................................................................29

CHAPTER 5: PRODUCT MANAGERS NEED NEW PRODUCT FLOP INSURANCE ..................................................................................34

CHAPTER 6: SHOULD A PRODUCT MANAGER BE A COPYCAT?..........39

CHAPTER 7: HEY PRODUCT MANAGER, CARE FOR SOME RISK?........43

CHAPTER 8: HOW PRODUCT MANAGERS CAN INNOVATE & NOT LOSE THEIR SHIRTS ...............................................................................48

CHAPTER 9: FAST PRODUCT MANAGEMENT LESSONS FROM A PORSCHE 911 ...............................................................................52

CHAPTER 10: PRODUCT MANAGEMENT MISTAKE: KEEPING BUSY IS HOW THINGS GET DONE ...............................................................57

CHAPTER 11: WHY PRODUCT MANAGERS NEED TO NOT FOLLOW THEIR DEVELOPMENT PLANS.........................................................62

CHAPTER 12: WHAT EVERY PRODUCT MANAGER NEEDS TO KNOW ABOUT THE HADOOP DATABASE SOLUTION..................................66

## It's All About The Product

As product managers it is our responsibility to create products that our customers will want and that will end up being profitable for our companies. It turns out that this is no easy task. Identifying what a customer really wants and then turning that into a feature that can be delivered to a customer is hard work. The key to being successful is to understand exactly what goes into world-class product development.

Every product uses some form of technology no matter if the technology is embedded in the product or if it is used to create the product. Product managers play a key role in selecting the correct technologies to use. Any product requires the company to make an investment in it. One aspect of this investment that is important to a product manager is the cost of capital. That money will be spent creating a product team. As product managers we need to realize that we'll have team members of different ages and we need to know how best to manage them all.

As we look around different industries, we look for examples that we can follow when developing products. The competition between Yahoo and Google in the area of financial reporting provides us with some good examples of what to do and what not to do. Because creating a new product is such a risky undertaking, we need to look for ways to hedge our bets. One thing that can reduce our risk is to copy something that someone else has already done. We need to keep in mind the amount of risk that will be involved.

Innovation is the key to creating new products that your customers will want. Examples from companies like Porsche can provide us with suggestions on how to go about doing this. The plan that we create to deliver a new product is just that – a plan. We need to make sure that we take action despite what the plan says in order to make sure that our product is delivered on time. New technologies, such as the Hadoop database, may play a key role in our ability to accomplish this.

For more information on what it takes to be a great product manager, check out my blog, The Accidental Product Manager, at:

**www.TheAccidentalPM.com**


Good luck!


- Dr. Jim Anderson

## About The Author

I must confess that I never set out to be a product manager. When I went to school, I studied Computer Science and thought that I'd get a nice job programming and that would be that. Well, at least part of that plan worked out!

My first job was working for Boeing on their F/A-18 fighter jet program. I spent my days programming fighter jet software in assembly language and I loved it. The U.S. government decided to save some money and went looking for other countries to sell this plane to. This put me into an unfamiliar role: I started to meet with foreign military officials in order to explain what my product did.

Time moved on and so did I. I found myself working for Siemens, the big German telecommunications company. They were making phone switches and selling them to the seven U.S. phone companies. The problem was that the switches were too complicated. Customers couldn't tell the difference between one complicated phone switch from another complicated phone switch.

The Siemens sales folks were in a bind. They didn't know enough about how the switches worked to tell their customers why they should buy them. Siemens reached out into their engineering unit looking for anyone who could help the sales teams out. I put my hand up and overnight I became a product manager.

Since then I've spent over 20 years working as a product manager for both big companies and startups. This has given me an opportunity to do everything that a product manager does many, many times. I know what works as well as what doesn't work.

I now live in Tampa Florida where I spend my time managing my consulting business, Blue Elephant Consulting, teaching college courses at the University of South Florida, and traveling to work with companies like yours to share the knowledge that I have about how product managers can make their product be a success.

I'm always available to answer questions and I can be reached at:

Dr. Jim Anderson
Blue Elephant Consulting
Email: jim@BlueElephantConsulting.com
Facebook: http://goo.gl/1TVoK
Web: **www.BlueElephantConsulting.com**

**"Unforgettable communication skills that will set your ideas free…"**

# Create Products Your Customers Want At A Price That They Are Willing To Pay!

Dr. Jim Anderson is available to provide training and coaching on the two topics that are the most important to product managers everywhere: how do I create the products that my customers want and what should I price them at?

Dr. Anderson believes that in order to both learn and remember what he says, product managers need to laugh. Each one of his speeches is full of fun and humor so that what he says "sticks" with everyone.

### Dr. Anderson's Product Management Training Includes:

1. How can you segment your market?
2. What problems are your customers having right now?
3. Which of your customer's problems does your product solve?
4. How much of this problem does your product solve?
5. How much will it cost your customer if they don't fix this problem?

Dr. Jim Anderson presents over 100 speeches per year. To invite Dr. Anderson to speak at your event, contact him at:

Phone: 813-418-6970  or
Email: jim@BlueElephantConsulting.com

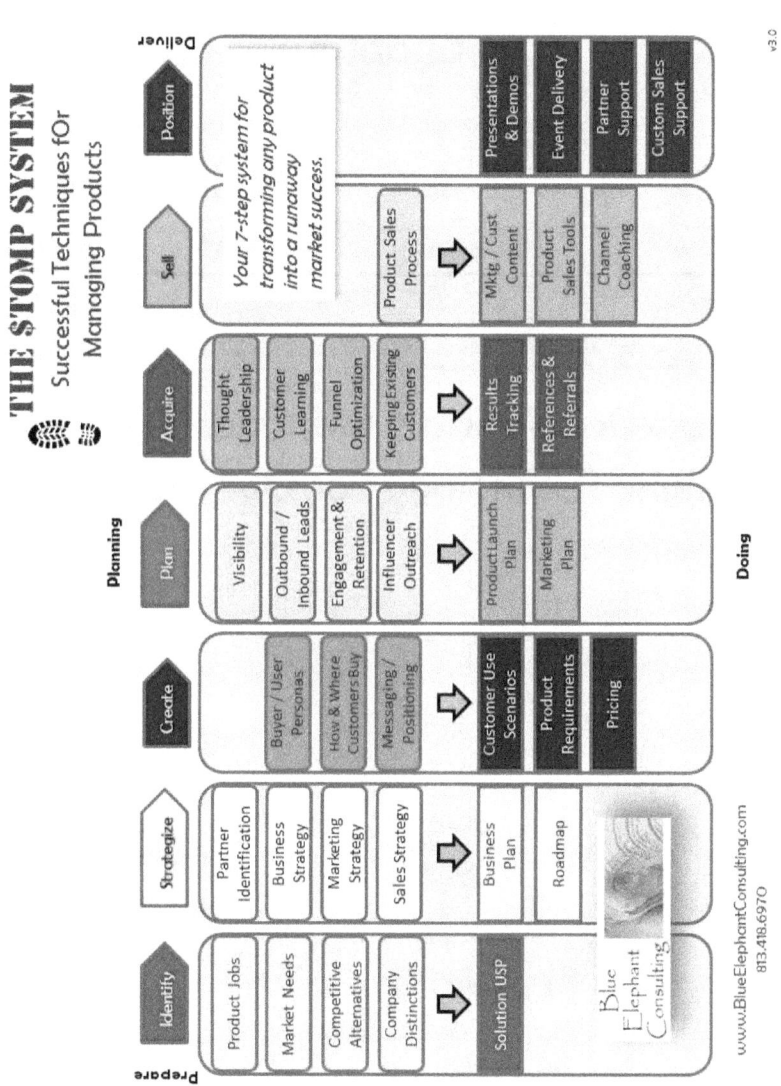

The **$TOMP** product management system has been created by **Blue Elephant Consulting** to help product managers know what to do and when to do it in order for a product to be successful.

# Chapter 1

## How Can Product Managers Pick The Right Technology For Our Products?

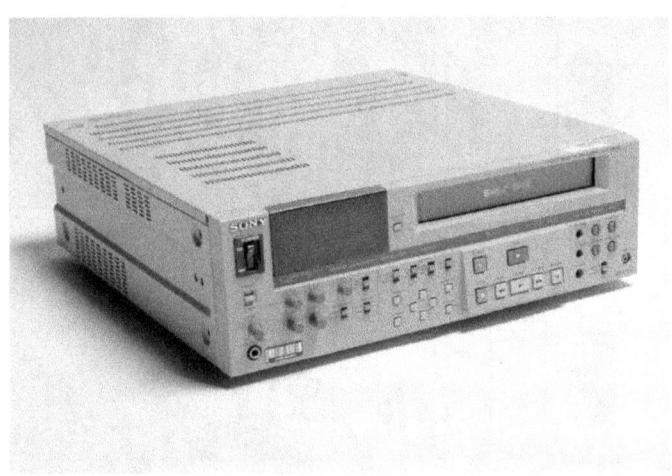

# Chapter 1: How Can Product Managers Pick The Right Technology For Our Products?

Just imagine if you were a movie studio executive back in the early 1980's: what format should you release your new movie on for the home market – VHS or Beta? Both technologies were battling it out and it was very difficult to try to predict a winner. That was a long time ago (by the way, VHS won), but product managers today still face the same challenge of trying to make sure that their product uses the correct next generation technology.

The names have changed, C++ vs C#, Java vs .NET, Adobe vs Silverlight, but the dilemma remains the same: how do you make the right decision when you can't see the future? Well Dr. Gerard Tellis and Dr. Ashish Sood have spent some time looking at how to do this and they've come away with some surprising (to me) insights.

One of their biggest discoveries is that we seem to do a lousy job of trying to distinguish between the different levels associated with a given technology. What this means is that we'll spend too much time looking at one level of a technology and then we'll get whacked in the back of the head when something changes on a different level.

The Dr's believe that each technology actually has three separate levels of what they call "technological innovation": platform, design, and component. The platform level is the underlying technology. An example is the LCD platform used in TVs.

The design and component levels of a technology is what we often spend our time looking at. This is because it is where the rapid innovation is occurring as companies try to leap past each other.

Finally, the platform level sees very little change normally, but when things do change, it can turn the world upside down. The arrival of thin & light LCD displays was a platform change that put the CRT manufactures out of business almost overnight.

# Chapter 2

# Product Managers Need To Know What Their Company's Cost Of Capital Is

# Chapter 2: Product Managers Need To Know What Their Company's Cost Of Capital Is

You've just been put in charge of managing the best product ever. Based on the product development definition, you know that this product is going to be a run-away success: it solves a critical problem that a lot of customers are currently facing. There's just one problem: either the product does not yet exist or it exists, but doesn't do what it needs to do. **You're going to need some money** – what's it going to take to get your company to fund your product?

## What Is The "Cost Of Capital"?

One of the things that too many product managers forget is that **their company does not HAVE to fund their product**. Yes, we can get all caught up in the fantastic market potential of our product, but from the company's perspective there are a lot of other things that they can do with their money.

What this means is that when you go asking for the funding that you are going to need in order to make your product successful, you are going to have to convince some people that your product represents **the best place for the company to spend its money**. This means that you're going to have to have a talk about the cost of capital. Figure this one out and you'll have something else to add to your product manager resume.

Generally speaking, the company's finance department is going to be in charge of **running the numbers on your request for funding**. What we product managers don't often realize is that the company many not have the money that we're requesting just sitting around. Instead, in order to fund our product, the company may need to dip into both its cash reserves (equity) as well as going out and borrowing some money.

Exactly how they go about doing this is something that too many product managers take a hands-off approach to. I'm going to suggest that we spend a little time talking about what you need to know about your cost of capital so that you've got the best chance of **getting the funding that you want**.

## 6 Assumptions Your Company Makes About Their Cost Of Capital

The world of finance can be mysterious to many product managers. However, with a little investigation you can quickly learn enough to be able to have a good discussion with your colleagues in the finance department. Here are **6 assumptions** that your finance team may be making about how much the capital for your project is going to cost the company:

1. **Investment Time Horizon:** We all know what this one is: how long after they give you the money is your product going to start to make money for the company? All too often a finance department has one set value that they use for this (1 year, 5 years, etc.). However, the investment time horizon should vary according to your product: innovative products will take longer to generate a profit than line extensions.

2. **How Much Does Debt Cost?:** When the folks in finance are trying to determine how much it's going to cost the company to borrow the money that they'll spend on your product, they need to find a benchmark to use. All too often a finance department will use the current average rate on outstanding debt. This is the wrong way to do it. They really need to be using the forecasted rate on new debt issuance. Make sure that they're doing it the right way!

3. **The Risk-Free Rate:** When trying to determine how much of a return your product should generate, finance people generally start by trying to determine how much of a return an investor would want to get from a risk-free investment. What this means is that they take a look at how much the U.S. Treasury is paying on investments. However, this is where the problem can pop up: which U.S. Treasury rate will they be looking at: the 10-year rate, the 5-year rate, or the 30-year bond? Make sure that when your request for funding gets compared to other requests, that an apples-to-apples risk-free rate rates are being used.

4. **Equity Market Premium:** Because investing in any project is risky, your finance department will be determining a risk premium for the funding that you are requesting. Many companies use a number between 5%-6%. However, this is probably an old number that hasn't been changed in a long time. Take a look and see if you think that it should go down. If so, have a talk with your finance department.

5. **Beta:** The volatility of your company's stock plays a role in how much equity is going cost. A beta that is greater than 1 means that the company has greater-than-average volatility. A beta less than 1 means that your company has less-than-average volatility. Where a product manager may run into problems is when your finance department can't agree on what time frame to measure the company's volatility over: 1 year, 2 years, 3 years, or 5 years?

6. **Debt-To-Equity Ratio:** It turns out that your product may be financed by a mixture of cash that the company has (equity) and debt. How much of each to use is something that the finance department needs to determine. The problem is that they often can't decide

if they should base this decision on the company's current book debt, targeted book debt, or current market debt. Picking the wrong one can drive your cost of capital way up.

7. **Risk Of The Product:** The final factor in determining the cost of capital for your product is to come up with an overall risk factor for your product. If the company takes a look at another product with a comparable level of risk, then they are doing it correctly. However, if they just tack on a percentage point to the value that they've already calculated for your cost of capital then they are doing it wrong. Find out how your finance team is coming up with this number!

## What All Of This Means For You

The next time that you are handed a product to manage, you need to review your product manager job description and take a careful look at what you are being given. There are probably some changes that need to be made to your product in order for it to truly be successful. This means that **you are going to need to get some company funding**.

In order to get the funding that you need, you're going to have to work with the company's finance department. **They'll be using the company's cost of capital to make funding decisions about your product**. This means that you are going to have to use the 6 techniques that we've discussed to make sure that they are using the correct cost of capital.

The world of finance can appear to be strange and intimidating to an uneducated product manager. That's why you need to learn about the cost of capital and then sit down and talk with your finance department in order to **ensure that you're going to get the best deal possible** for your product. If you are going to be a successful product manager, then you're going to have to know how to speak the language of finance.

# Chapter 3

# How Product Managers Can Manage The Age Gap On Their Product Teams

# Chapter 3: How Product Managers Can Manage The Age Gap On Their Product Teams

Product managers often don't manage any direct reports. However, in order to have a successful product, we always seem to find ourselves **in charge of a sort of "virtual team" of people** who are sprinkled throughout the company. It turns out that in order for our product to be a success, we need to do a good job of managing this virtual team. That means that we've got to find a way to deal with the age gap issue…

## Where Did The Age Gap Come From?

Once you get done creating your product development definition, it's time to manage the workers who make up your product's virtual team. This won't always be the case, but for right now **we've got three different generations of workers that make up our teams**. First off, there are the so called "Baby Boomers" who were born 1946-1964 – these are the older members of your team. Next comes the "Generation X" workers who were born between 1964 – 1980. Finally you have the newest set of workers who are called the Millennials and they were born between 1980-2000. Good luck getting all of them to work together to make your product a success!

The big problem for a product manager is that each one of these groups likes to **communicate in a different way** and they all respond to different types of motivations. Clearly, there is not one solution that is going to get them all on board when it comes to your product. If you can come up with a solution to this problem, then you'll have something to add to your product manager resume.

## How Should Product Managers Handle The Age Gap

The first issue that you are going to have to deal with as a product manager is uncovering **how each generational group wants to be communicated with**. The answer is going to depend on what communication tools they grew up with and are most comfortable using. The Baby Boomers like using both the telephone and face-to-face communication. The Gen X workers are more comfortable using email and instant messaging. Finally, the Millennials prefer to use their smart phones and communicate using social media applications such as Facebook and Twitter.

What each generation **wants to get out of their job** (and working on your product) will differ also. The older members of your virtual product team will have more work experience in more traditional hierarchical organizations. The younger members will be more familiar with flatter organizations where they believe that they can contribute and that their voices will be heard. Note that this can lead to clashes where your older workers believe that the right to be heard has to be earned over time.

As a product manager it's going to be your responsibility to **discover how each member of your product's virtual team wants to communicate** and what they want to get out of working on your product. This means that the burden of discovering this information is on you to find out. Once you have this information you can start to tailor how you communicate with the rest of the team in order to make sure that your message and your requests are being received and understood by the people that you need to take action.

## What Does All Of This Mean For You

It would be a perfect world in if everyone that worked on your product's "virtual team" was exactly the same. However, the world is not perfect and you've got three different generations of workers to deal with on your team even if that was never a part of your product manager job description.

The Baby Boomers, Generation X, and Millennials all have different ways of communicating. Additionally, they are looking to get different things out of their jobs. As product manager you need to discover what these things are and then use them to connect with the members of your team.

It's not going to be easy and there may be people who belong to one generation who like to do things the way that another generation does it. That's ok. You need to take the time to find out how your product's team wants to interact with you and then you need to use that information. Keep in mind that your product is only going to be as successful as the team that works on it is. Learn what they want, give it to them, and watch them work to make your product a success.

# Chapter 4

# How Yahoo Product Managers Are Kicking Google's Butt

# Chapter 4: How Yahoo Product Managers Are Kicking Google's Butt

If you had the choice of being a product manager at either Yahoo or Google, which company would you choose? I'm going to go out on a limb and say that most of us would choose to work at **Google**.

The press is filled with glowing stories about how great everything that Google touches is. Of course, there's the **free food at work** angle also. Likewise, Yahoo has been getting savaged in the press as they lose visitors, botch marketing agreements with Microsoft, and generally drop the ball.

However, it turns out that we might be making the wrong decision. In the battle for capturing viewers for financial information, the Yahoo product managers are **winning the battle** hands down…

## Statistics Don't Lie

Randall Stross over at the New York Times has taken a close look the ongoing battle between Google and Yahoo for Web users who are looking for timely financial news. You might think that things are close or that Google is coming on strong. You'd be wrong. Right now Yahoo's financial site is attracting **17.5x the traffic** that Google's financial site is getting. You read that correctly: not 2x, not 10x, but 17.5x!

This is not a recent occurrence either. For the last **19 months** (1.6 years if you care) Yahoo Finance has been #1 in this category. Google is currently ranked 17th. Yahoo was able to attract 21.7M unique visitors while Google has only been able to attract 1.2M unique visitors.

## What Yahoo Product Mangers Are Doing Right

In talking with Yahoo's product managers Stross found that they had taken the time to sit down with their target audience and discover what they wanted – and what they didn't want. This research revealed that the more financial information that was presented to users, the **greater their anxiety became**.

Once the Yahoo product team had this break-through realization, they went ahead and took a page out of Apple's product playbook and created a very simple design that had a clean look that **didn't overload** the visitor with too much information.

The Yahoo team also realized that one of their greatest assets was **other Yahoo sites**. The Yahoo Finance team developed a great relationship with the Yahoo's front page team and they have worked together to identify what topics the Finance team could cover that would allow the front page team to send traffic to them.

Yahoo has achieved this product success with very little original content. In fact, only about 5% of the Yahoo Finance site's information is original. Yahoo realizes that this is a weakness and they plan on boosting this to 10% in the future.

## Does Google Have The Better Product?

Does anyone remember the VHS vs. Beta video tape format wars that happened so many years ago? It sure looks like we are looking at a repeat of this once again. Google arguably has a **technically superior financial site.**

Goggle's strategy so far has been to offer visitors the **best financial data and charts**. In the case that this is not enough, Google comes back and offers them even more data and charts.

One of the biggest drawbacks that the Google Finance team has is that Google's home page **does not have a clear link** to the Google Finance page. It's entirely possible that a visitor to the Google home page may never learn that the Google Finance page even exists because the only reference to it is buried in a list of menu items.

One clear advantage that Google has over the Yahoo Finance page is that they offer **free real-time price quotations** obtained directly from the New York Stock Exchange and Nasdaq. Yahoo Finance on the other hand gets its stock prices from the BATS Exchange and they have a delay of roughly 1 minute.

Google visitors get real-time stock prices for free, Yahoo visitors **have to pay** for access to real-time quotes – $10.95 or $13.95 / month (NYSE or Nasdaq).

### Final Thoughts

Who's going to win this battle? You would think that that with Google's deep pockets they would eventually come out the victor. However, it appears as though Google's product managers **still don't get it**.

A case in point is Google's new set of stock price charting tools that they call "**Technicals**". These tools allow users to analyze stock prices over time using 12 different technical formulas. Based on what Yahoo has discovered about visitors to financial information pages, this new set of features will not boost Google's draw.

In the end, the product managers at Yahoo Finance understand that the best way for a free financial site to prosper is by including less mathematics and **more entertainment**. The winner of this battle will inform their users just enough to answer their questions without causing them any unnecessary anxiety.

Product managers at Yahoo who are able to stay tuned into what their finance customers are really looking for will have found yet another way that great product managers make their product(s) **fantastically successful**.

# Chapter 5

# Product Managers Need New Product Flop Insurance

# Chapter 5: Product Managers Need New Product Flop Insurance

Is there any part of a product manager's job that is more exciting than being responsible for introducing a new product? For that matter, is there any experience that can be more nerve racking than introducing a new product? If only there was some way that we could take out "flop insurance" that would help to prevent our becoming known as the product manager who introduced the next "new Coke" disaster...

## Why New Product Fail

In 2003 34,000 new products were introduced. 90% of them failed. In 2008 122,743 new products were introduced and the failure rate was about 80%. Those odds **don't look so good** for your next new product introduction, do they?

Dr. Rita Gunther McGrath has been studying the tools that companies use to plan for new product launches and she thinks that she knows what we've been doing wrong. It turns out that **we've been using the wrong tools**.

## What's Wrong With The Way That We've Been Doing Things?

As any product manager who has spent any time working for a large firm knows, there is **no shortage** of tools available to help product managers plan for the introduction of a new product. It turns out that most of these tools no longer work correctly.

The problem is caused by the simple fact that things have changed. A lot. Most of the tools that are currently available to product managers are based on an assumption that what's happened in the past can be used to predict what will happen in the future. Now that most of the markets that we design new products for are **moving so quickly**, these assumptions are no longer valid.

## Is There A Better Way To Plan For A New Product Launch?

Thankfully, yes there is a better way. Dr. McGrath proposes that we start to use what she calls "**discovery driven growth**". This approach is basically a plan for learning more as the launch process moves forward. The part that I like about this way of doing things is that it doesn't require the product manager to have a lot of analytical information at the start of the launch process. In my opinion that's a good idea simply because there generally isn't a lot of information available!

## What Makes This Approach Different?

So in the graveyard of products that were bad ideas from the start (e.g. New Coke, Pets.com, etc.) **what went wrong?** These products had bright, smart product managers running the show and they created elaborate, beautiful plans that they followed to the letter when launching their products.

It turns out that they did **two things** wrong and these conspired to cause them to fail. The first was that they started with untested assumptions and then used them as facts on which they built their launch plans.

The second thing that they did wrong is that they built **a false reality** that blocked out the truth. They built products, and then second generation products, they launched advertising programs, etc. They did so much work that it all started to seem real to them, when in fact everything was built on some bad guesses about what the market really wanted.

## What Is The Right Way To Launch A Product?

Dr. McGrath says that what we should do is to start any launch process by **writing down** what our assumptions are as we are creating the business plan. Overtime we'll forget what our assumptions are.

Next you need to **identify the milestones** that you'll be reaching as you get closer and closer to launching your new product. Once the milestones are known, you need to determine which of your assumptions you'll revisit at that milestone in order to determine if they are still valid.

The ultimate goal of this is to spot when any assumptions are found to be **no longer be valid** as early in the process as possible. You may end up killing the new product, but you'll save the company a lot of money.

## What All Of This Means For You

Launching a new product is the **ultimate thrill** for a product manager. If successful it can make your career. Likewise, if it's a flop then there is a good chance that your career at your company may be over and done with.

One of the biggest problems that product managers face when launching new products is that the planning tools that we use are **out-of-date**. They assume that the future will be like the past, and that just ain't true anymore.

Using the discovery-driven growth approach allows product managers to document what their initial assumptions were and to **revisit them** during the launch process. This allows any fundamentally wrong assumptions to be detected as early as possible and corrective action (including killing the product) to be taken.

Launching a new product is never easy. However, this new approach to launch planning just might make it **turn out successful more often!**

# Chapter 6

---

# Should A Product Manager Be A Copycat?

# Chapter 6: Should A Product Manager Be A Copycat?

Every product manager dreams of his / her product turning into the next iPhone, or Google search engine, or some other runaway success like that. However, as we all too well know, the odds of that ever happening are actually pretty slim. However, maybe there's another way to become successful and famous. Maybe the key to Product Management stardom is not in being an innovator, but rather in being a really, really good copycat?

## You Mean I'm Allowed To Copy Off Of Others?

Would you like to know an ugly little secret? Dr. Oded Shenkar has been studying this area and he's discovered that roughly 97.8% of the ultimate value that an innovation creates will end up going to the imitator firms, not the inventor firm.

Dr. Shenkar also points out that the world of copycats is moving even faster these days. In the old days it took a long time to copy someone else's product, now not so long. A case in point is the mini-van that was invented by Chrysler back in the 1980's. It was another 10 years before another car company came out with an imitation. On the other hand, CD players were imitated after only 3 years.

## Just Making A Copy Isn't Enough

Before you run off to go buy a copy of whatever your competition is making so that you can start to stamp out clones of it, you might want to wait for just a minute. Making exact copies of someone else's product is going to get you in trouble with the patent office and it's not going to help you to be successful.

What a copycat product manager needs to realize is that it's not enough to copy another product; you actually need to improve on it. This is where things get difficult.

In order to find the right products to copy, a product manager needs to be constantly searching for the next candidate to copy. Where this product is going to be found is never clear – you may have to search far and wide in multiple industries to find what you are looking for.

Once you find a product that would be a good fit for your company to copy, your work as a product manager is just beginning. What needs to be done now is to understand what the core essence of the product to be copied is: why do people like it / use it / want it? What you are going to need to do is to create a way to make it cheaper, better, or faster than the original firm.

## Why Aren't More Product Managers Copycats?

Given that all of the evidence points to the simple fact that product managers who are good at copying what others have done end up being more successful leads to a simple question: why don't more of us do this?

It turns out that the answer to this question is pretty simple: we've been conditioned to think of being a copycat as being "wrong". Most firms like to think of themselves as being innovators, not as being imitators.

Too often we view the process of creating a copy of an existing product as being in some way undignified. What we're missing is that if you are taking an original idea and then improving on it, you are well on your way to product success.

## What All Of This Means For You

Apple is a great company that comes up with really innovative products such as the iPad. However, time will show that most of the value of the iPad won't go to Apple – instead it will go to firms that create and deploy copycat products that do a better job than the iPad does.

Although most firms don't like to think of themselves as being imitators instead of innovators, this is where the real value is. The secret is to make sure that you don't just create a copy of a product, but rather that you improve on the original in a way that will make it even more attractive to potential customers.

The key to being a successful imitator product manager is to learn to keep your eyes open. Where the next product that you can improve on will be found is always a mystery. To win the race to deliver a successful product, you don't have to be first, you just have to be the best.

# Chapter 7

# Hey Product Manager, Care For Some Risk?

# Chapter 7: Hey Product Manager, Care For Some Risk?

Every product that you are put in charge of developing comes with an unwelcome addition – **risk**. We all know that risk exists and in fact many of us have developed ways to identify risk, quantify risk, and even manage risk. However it turns out that there is something very important that very few of us have been doing – calculating how much risk a new product has and what it's going to cost us.

## Why You've Been Calculating Product Development Risk All Wrong

I can only speak for myself here, but when I'm placed in charge of creating a new product, the thing that I really don't want to be thinking about is risk. Rather, I prefer to focus on just exactly **how I'm going to accomplish what I'm being asked to do**. It turns out that in this case, I'm probably wrong.

Every new product has some level of risk associated with it. It makes sense that as product managers we really should **be aware** of how much risk developing a given product has. Look, our careers are riding on this stuff and it sure seems as though we should go into it with our eyes wide open instead of squeezing them shut and hoping for the best.

Paul Armour is a consultant who has been looking into such things. What he's discovered is that we've been taking the easy way out when it comes to calculating the risk of developing a new product. If we're not careful, this kind of over simplifying is going to end up coming back and biting us.

What we've been doing is saying things like, "it's going to cost US$10M to develop and launch this new product." We then follow this up with another statement like "this product will generate US$500k in profit in the next 2 years. If we don't worry about all of that time-value-of-money stuff, we then go on to say that the **return-on-investment (ROI)** of creating this new product is 500k / 10M = 0.05 or about 5%.

Here's what's wrong with this approach: you don't know that it's going to cost US$10M to launch the product (it may take more) and you don't know that it's going to generate US$500k in profits (it may bring in less). These two points are what we call **the risk associated with this new product development**.

## How To Correctly Calculate The Risk Of Product Development

So now that you know that what you've been doing all along when it comes to calculating the risk associated with new projects is wrong, what should you be doing? The first thing that you need to do is to find a way to work risk into your **view of the world**.

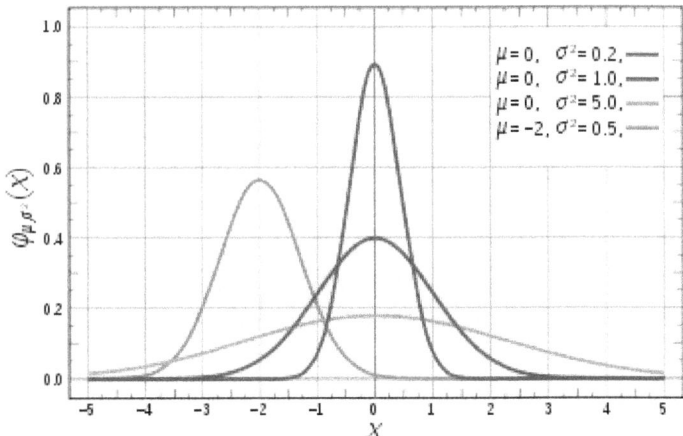

In a normal distribution you can see that the risk profile of a new product development process can take on **many different**

**shapes**. The traditional shape would be a straight line that reached up to 1.0 – basically a 100% chance that the project would complete on budget and would produce the expected profits.

A normal distribution shows **a more accurate real-world view**. If the X-axis shows how much you've invested in the new product and the Y-axis shows the probability of completing the project on time and making the expected level of profit, then you can start to see how much risk you are dealing with.

In no case will you ever have a 100% guarantee that you'll be able to stay within your budget or **achieve profit goals**. Some projects are more likely that others to overrun their budgets (you know what products I'm talking about here).

In the end, Armour has identified **6 different issues** that product managers need to consider when we are trying to accurately calculate the amount of risk that there is in developing and launching a new product:

1. Expected cost of the project

2. Probability of being able to stay within that expected cost

3. What the graph of the budget risk profile looks like

4. Expected profitability of the new product

5. Probability of being able to achieve the expected profit

6. What the graph of the profit risk profile looks like

In the end, every product manager has a responsibility to know what the **level of risk** associated with the creation of a new product is. What you choose to do with this knowledge is your own business, but you need to make sure that you know what you are dealing with.

## What All Of This Means For You

Product managers live in **a world filled with risk**. Although we all know this, it can be easy to forget it at times and take the simple route in which we don't correctly calculate just how much risk we are facing when we start to develop a new product.

Our problems often stem from the fact that all too often we end up making **simplifying assumptions** that just aren't valid. The two most common points that we seem to overlook when we are evaluating if we should develop a new product include forgetting to factor in our ability to complete the development on time and on budget as well as the ability of the product to generate the profits that we think that it will.

Taking the time to account for both of these risks will give product managers a more **realistic view of the world** that they live in. What we end up doing with this new information is our own decision; however, there is no excuse for us to not have the information in the first place.

# Chapter 8

# A New Way For Product How Product Managers Can Innovate & Not Lose Their Shirts

# Chapter 8: How Product Managers Can Innovate & Not Lose Their Shirts

What's your plan for **making your product a success going forward?** Hoping some magic fairy shows up and makes your competition go away overnight? Well good luck with that! I suspect that your management is probably pressing you and your product team to do some of that "innovation" stuff. Got any ideas on how to make it happen?

## The Two Flavors Of Innovation

We all think that we know what innovation is, but do we really? We view innovation as being the process by which **successful products** get invented like the iPhone, the Kindle, etc. However, those product teams have access to some sort of magic pixy dust that the rest of us can't touch. How are we supposed to use innovation to make our products better?

Really smart people, like Dr. Rosabeth Moss Kanter, have taken a close look at this innovation thing and they've discovered that **not all innovation is created the same**.

What they've found is that there are actually **two different types of innovation**. The first is what we're all familiar with: the blockbuster breakthrough thought. This is the kind of thinking that produced the iPad. Not bad – if only product managers could have these types of thoughts every day!

Thankfully there is another type of innovation. This is the **incremental change type of innovation**. It's a much smaller type of breakthrough, but we have a lot more of them and they turn out to be just as important.

For you see, the **blockbuster breakthroughs** are built on top of a whole bunch of incremental breakthroughs. In fact, the researchers have discovered that you really can't have a blockbuster breakthrough if you don't have a bunch of incremental breakthroughs in order to support the blockbuster.

## How To Innovate With Your Product

I can almost hear you saying, "oh great, so now not only do I have to have blockbuster innovations, but now I also have a bunch of incremental innovations…" **Well, yes and no**.

Instead of getting all tied up in knots about what you do or don't have to do in order to innovate with your product, it might be simpler to **implement a framework** for allowing innovation to happen.

One way to do this is to look at innovations as they relate to your product as being organized **in a pyramid fashion**. At the base of the pyramid are all of the little ideas that are always popping up about how the product can be improved. These can come from anywhere: internally or from customers.

The ideas that are "no-brainers" need to be **implemented right away**. The ones that will require some time and investment, but which look promising should be thought of as moving to the next layer of the innovation pyramid.

At this level, investments are made, changes happen, and innovation starts to **become apparent** in different parts of the product if you look at it hard enough. Nothing revolutionary, but the product does keep getting better.

The final stage of the pyramid is the top. This is where **the big ideas** get kicked up to. These ideas require the product manager and the firm to make a big bet on where the world is headed. If your senior management agrees, these ideas are the ones that will create the breakthrough innovations for your product that everyone will be talking about.

## What All Of This Means For You

Since you are responsible for the success of your product, you need to make sure that both you and your team **keep innovating** and making the product better and better. That means that you're going to have to find ways to make innovation happen.

It turns out that there is **more than one type of innovation**. There are the big innovations that get all of the press and then there are the incremental innovations that are needed to allow the big innovations happen.

Product managers need to **implement a framework** that allows innovative ideas to be collected into a pyramid of innovation that will allow good ideas to be implemented no matter if they are small, medium, or breakthrough in size.

Innovation is a core requirement for every product – every product has a half-life and you need to be adding value to it in order to **ensure its success**. Use this deeper understanding of innovation to show your management and the market that your product is the most innovative.

# Chapter 9

## Fast Product Management Lessons From A Porsche 911

# Chapter 9: Fast Product Management Lessons From A Porsche 911

This is the kind of story that I really like – **it has a Porsche in it!** Hopefully everyone knows who Porsche is. They are the German car manufacturer who makes ridiculously fast sports cars and then sells them for an awful lot of money. It's how they go about doing the selling part that just might hold some lessons for Product Managers...

## Behold: the Porsche 911!!

What kind of car do you drive today? I'm willing to bet that it's nothing like the brand new Porsche that was recently introduced. This car is a beast. It has 394 horsepower under the hood and **can go from 0 – 60 m.p.h. in 4 seconds**. Ouch – who needs that kind of power? Wouldn't we all like to be able to add that kind of product to our product manager resume?

It really doesn't matter who needs that kind of power, because we all simply want it! Unfortunately as with all things in life, automobile power comes at a price. In this case **the price of nicely outfitted Porsche 911 is roughly US$132,360**.

Even though the product, the 911, is a highly desirable one, the product managers at Porsche realize that the people who make up their market segment do **have other options** when it comes to high end sports cars. This means that they need to take steps to cause people to choose a Porsche when they go expensive car shopping.

All too often we product managers try to find different ways to talk about our products so that they will seem to have a little bit of everything for everyone. The most important thing that the Porsche product managers have realized is that **it's just not** possible to make one product that is going to meet every potential customer's needs.

## What Porsche Product Managers Know About Product Lines

The Porsche product managers have clearly started in the right place. Since they know that they can't capture every customer with a single product, they've decided to **create multiple variations of a single popular product**. The thinking is that if you like the base product, then once they create a variant that exactly matches what you are looking for you'll be almost forced to buy one.

How could the Porsche product managers make the apparently perfect 911 even better than it currently is? **How about if they made multiple models?** The last version of the Porsche 911 came in 18 configurations that were grouped in four main categories:

- **Turbo:** This configuration allowed the 911 to accelerate faster.

- **GT3:** This was a configuration that improved the 911's handling at high speeds.

- **GT3 RS:** This was a configuration of the 911 that was created for racing at such events as Sebring and the 24 Hours of Le Mans.

- **GT2:** A street-legal configuration that accelerates faster and breaks even quicker.

The latest version of the 911 clearly shows that over at Porsche they know all about the product development definition. This means that the Porsche product managers have a product roadmap and **they are in the process of executing it**. The just introduced model has spare room designed in around the engine that will permit a larger engine to be added to future models. Additionally, since this version of the 911 is both longer and has a wider wheelbase, it is anticipated that there will be a hybrid version in the not so distant future.

Instead of having to scramble to adapt the current product design to handle some last minute **"must have" feature**, it's pretty clear that the Porsche product managers have a long-term product roadmap and that they are executing it. This kind of planning and execution is something that all product managers could learn a thing or two from.

## What All Of This Means For You

I want a Porsche 911. Of course, so does everyone else so that's not really saying very much. However, the product managers at Porsche know that we all want their car and they've taken steps to make sure that every last person who can possibly buy their car **will do so**. This is the kind of product management skill that should be in every product manager job description

The Porsche 911 is a fantastic piece of machinery. It looks great and it drives like a bat out of hell. However, it's only going to get better. The Porsche product managers have **pre-engineered this beast** to be able to be transformed into multiple future models: bigger, faster, and perhaps even a hybrid. What this means is that they have already thought out their product development roadmap and even as you read this they are working on the future.

Taking the time to plan not just the next version of your product, but the next next and even the next next next version can yield great rewards for a product manager. Let the success of the Porsche 911 show you the way to make sure that your next product launch **gets your product in the fast lane** so that you can put the petal to the metal...!

# Chapter 10

# Product Management Mistake: Keeping Busy Is How Things Get Done

# Chapter 10: Product Management Mistake: Keeping Busy Is How Things Get Done

Why is it so hard to create new products both on time and under budget? Your management ignores the product development definition process and is always pushing you to get it done while at the same time they never seem to give you enough resources to make it happen. When they push, what do you do? If you are like most of us, **you are probably reacting in the wrong way...**

## New Product Development Is Not Like Running A Factory

All too often other parts of the company can view the job of being a product manager as being like the person who is **running a factory** that produces products. The problem with this view is that product management is NOT like running a factory – your product manager resume says nothing about you having factory skills.

A factory deals with the process of **making a physical object**. The tasks that are involved are repetitive and it's fairly easy to predict the activities that will be required to make the object. Additionally, the thing that is being made can really only be in one place at a time.

The world of product management **looks much different**. Many of the tasks that are involved in developing a product are unique. The requirements for our products are always changing. More often than not, the output of the product management process is information which has the ability to exist in multiple places at the same time.

The fact that these differences are not always appreciated leads many firms and their product managers to **making mistakes**.

## The Big Utilization Mistake

At the company that you work at, there are a certain set of resources (generally people) that are involved in new product development. A big question is **how well utilized are these resources?** Unfortunately, many product managers try to keep these resources fully utilized all the time – think 98%.

The thinking goes something like this. It's going to take longer to develop that next product if the people who are supposed to be working on it aren't fully engaged. Therefore, if the product manager can **keep them 100% utilized**, then the next product will be created faster and more efficiently.

The problem with this kind of product manager thinking is that it simply **does not work out in real life**. Instead what happens is that a new product development effort will slow down, become less efficient, and the final quality will drop when the product development team is over utilized.

## The Right Way To Solve The Utilization Problem

We've all seen what can happen if a product development team gets too busy. **So what's the solution?** It turns out that there are four steps that a product manager can take to improve the new product development process without overloading the development team:

1. **Change How Things Are Measured:** Is it possible that you are measuring the wrong things? If you are keeping track of the utilization of team instead of its output, then you are playing the role of a program manager, not a product manager. Focus on having a team play well

with other teams and don't worry about individual member's utilization.

2. **Increase Capacity Where Needed:** Take a look at your product development process. Where are the utilizations over 70%? If you can add additional resources here, then you'll significantly reduce waiting times.

3. **Keep The Number Of Active Projects To A Minimum:** Although it might seem like a great idea to have as many projects being worked at the same time as possible, it turns out that it's not. Limiting the number of new products that are being developed at any given time will allow your development team to have a sharper focus and clearer priorities.

4. **Show What's Being Worked On:** Create a "dashboard" that will clearly show to everyone involved in the project just exactly what all of the different parts of the development team are doing. Make sure that this shows all of the active work and what state each part of the new product development project is in. By doing this you'll allow work to be coordinated and allow it to keep moving on.

## What All Of This Means For You

Product managers who are under pressure from their management are often tempted to push their development teams to **work harder**, create more detailed plans, and to minimize waste. All too often we think that this is part of our product manager job description. The problem with all of this is that it may not be solving the problem.

All too often product managers believe that if they can just keep their development resources **running at full utilization** (no vacations!) then they'll be able to deliver their product on time. For a number of reasons this never seems to work out.

Instead, product managers need to **align objectives**, selectively increase capacity, limit the number of projects, and make it easier to see the work that is being done.

Creating a new product will always be hard to do. Product managers need to take steps to ensure that **they are not making it even harder!**

1.

# Chapter 11

---

# Why Product Managers Need To Not Follow Their Development Plans

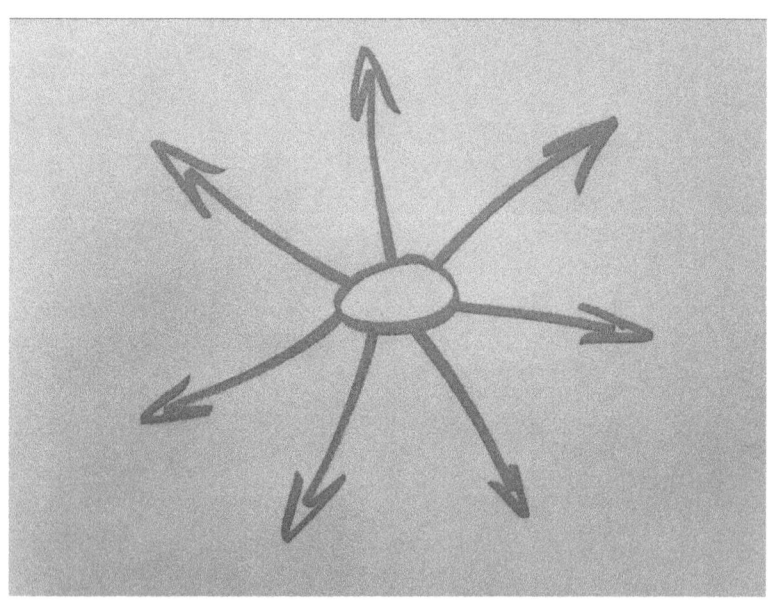

# Chapter 11: Why Product Managers Need To Not Follow Their Development Plans

If you got a chance to sit down with another product manager and share with them what you thought that they would have to do **in order to be successful**, what would you tell them? I'm thinking that a lot of us would tell them that they needed to make sure that once they came up with a development plan for their product, they needed to make sure that their team stuck with it. This is considered to be part of the product development definition. It turns out that this just might be the worst advice that you could give to a product manager...

## Why Sticking With Your Development Plan Is Wrong

I don't know about you, but when I'm managing a product I spend a lot of time on **crafting a development plan for that product**. I talk with everyone who will be involved in creating the product and I talk with customers all in an effort to collect all of the information that I'll need. When I'm done, I'm actually quite proud of the development plan that I've been able to create. This is the kind of skill that we all like to put on our product manager resume.

This is where the problem first starts to show up. The requirements that I've built my plan on **are not stable**. During the design process, these requirements are going to change. This is what can cause me to run into problems.

For you see, the rest of the world saw me putting the time and energy into creating my product development plan. What this means is that they, just like I, **now believe that it's perfect**. That means that if I start to deviate from it because requirements have changed, they'll see those deviations as being signs of poor management or poor execution.

What is too easy for both a product manager and their company to overlook is that the development of a product **is an innovative process**. For most products, new insights are being discovered on a daily basis and the market conditions will be changing all the time.

## Why Customers Can't Help You With Your Development Plan

Early on in my product management career, I had hopes that my customers **would show me the way** when I was developing a new product development plan. It turns out that all too often, this doesn't happen.

It is the responsibility of the product manager to attempt to define his or her customer's needs. At the start of product-development-project this can be very hard to do. The reason for this is very simple: your customers will have a very hard time trying to communicate their requirements **for a product that does not yet exist**.

What makes this situation even worse is that your customers will draw their needs based on **what they already know** – things that they are familiar with. This means that their needs and desires may change during your product development process as new products enter the market and as new customer trends show up.

## What All Of This Means For You

Does all of this mean that a product manager should not waste his or her time with bothering to come up with a product development plan? The answer to that question is no. Creating a product is a difficult thing to do and your product manager job description says that you need a plan in order to **coordinate the actions** of all of the people who will be involved.

However, it's **how you treat your product development plan** that may need to change. Instead of viewing it as being set in stone, instead view your plan as simply being a starting point.

What this means is that you need to be **constantly updating and revising your product development plan** as new things are discovered, your assumptions change, and the customer's situation is reevaluated. The success of your product depends on using your development plan correctly!

# Chapter 12

## What Every Product Manager Needs To Know About The Hadoop Database Solution

# Chapter 12: What Every Product Manager Needs To Know About The Hadoop Database Solution

Just in case you've been living with your head underneath a rock, the world appears to have gone **"big data" crazy** lately. Your customers, your company, and probably your competition have all started to talk about the problem of big data and just exactly what can be done about it. Somehow you are going to have to find a way to work "big data" into your product development definition. No matter what type of product you manage, it sure seems like you need to understand what this problem is – and how it can be solved.

## What's Wrong With How We Handle Data Today?

Before we go running off trying to solve a problem, let's first make sure that **we really have a problem that needs to be solved**. If you and I were going to create a database today, how would we go about doing it?

Let's say that we wanted to create a database to hold name and address information. The simplest way to think about a database is to **picture a table**. This table has both rows and columns. In our name and address database, we'll create a new row to hold your address information and we'll start out by creating a new column to hold your name. We'll then create 5 more columns and use each one to store one component of your home address: street, apartment number, city, state, and zip code (assuming that you live in the United States).

That's it! Now we have **a very small database**: it contains one record (yours) and that record holds 6 pieces of data: your name and your address. Now if we went one step further and added the names and addresses of everyone who lives in your town to this database it would grow from one record to now contain thousands of records, perhaps even millions of records depending on where you live.

Now imagine that you owned a flower shop in your town. One day you discover that you have too many roses. You'd like to send a postal letter to **everyone who lives in the area around your store** and remind them that a great way to say "I love you" is by giving someone roses. You don't want to send this email to everyone in town because if they live too far away they won't make the drive to your store and you'd just be wasting the money to send them the letter.

You can now go to our new database and **ask it a question**: please provide me with a list of all of the names and addresses for people whose address has the same area code as my store (this means that they live nearby). Once the database provides you with this list, you can go address all of your letters and sell your roses.

## Say Hello To The Hadoop Distributed File System

The type of database system that we just described has worked very well for the past 40 years. However, in the past 15 years **problems have started to show up because of big data**. A little company called Google was one of the first to run into this problem. Back in 2002, Google wanted to index the world wide web every day – talk about a lot data!

Let's think about **a challenging problem**. How about if we wanted to create a database that contained all of the data that was collected as a part of the last U.S. census. There are roughly 360M people living in the United States. If each answered 100 census questions, than that is a database with 360M rows and 100 columns – one big database!

Even if we were able to fit it onto a storage system that our little database engine from the last example could use, it would **take a week or more** to generate an answer to a question that we asked it. Don't even think about having multiple people use it at the same time. If you could figure out a way to solve this problem, then that would be something that you could add to your product manager resume.

A better way to handle big data was needed. A researcher named Doug Cutting stumbled across a couple of papers that Google had published that talked about how they had solved the problem of indexing an ever growing word wide web in a reasonable amount of time. Doug realized that with some work, he might be able to use these ideas to **create a database** that could handle very large data sets. With this idea, the Hadoop database system was born.

When it comes to big data, the first problem that has to be solved is **how to store all of that data**. No matter how you slice it, it's going to take a lot of hard drives. The Hadoop distributed file system tackles the problem in the following way.

The fundamental unit that makes up a Hadoop computer consists of **a "node"**. A node is a cheap processor, some memory, and one or more disk drives (generally hundreds of disk drives). Put a bunch of nodes together and you've got a "rack". Put a bunch of racks together and now you've got a "cluster".

First the data is broken up into 512k "storage units". Next these storage units are grouped together into 64k "file units". The file units are then stored on disks associated with a cluster. Since any disk in the cluster might fail at any time, multiple copies of each file unit (generally 3 copies) are stored on different disk drives at the same time. Although you are going to need to have a lot of disk drives, **you have now solved your storage problem for your big data**.

## Did Somebody Say MapReduce?

Having all of that data stored will do you no good if you can't **ask the Hadoop database questions** and get answers quickly. That's where the Hadoop MapReduce function comes in.

This function is responsible for taking your question, **splitting it up** and sending it to all of the clusters. There an answer is created for the cluster. MapReduce then collects all of the answers and reduces these answers down into a single answer which is then returned to you.

What this means is that the problem of searching a very large database has been transformed from a single big problem into **a set of distributed smaller problems**. Since each of the file units are exactly the same size, the operation will take the same amount of time in each cluster and you'll have your answer very quickly.

## What All Of This Means For You

Whew! That's a lot of database talk – what does a product manager care about all of this? No matter if your product can make use of a Hadoop database or if you are the one who is going to need to use a Hadoop database in order to process all of the product data that you collect and store, **Hadoop is eventually going to be part of your life**.

You might not be programming your product's Hadoop database, but you will be **interacting with the people who are**. You need to understand how the system works so that you'll be able to interpret what your database support team is telling you. Consider having a working knowledge of Hadoop to have been added to your product manager job description.

Take the time to do some studying and find out **what situations the Hadoop database is well suited for**. Work with your support team to make sure that they design a solution that is going to support your product's needs for both today as well as for tomorrow.

It's from the forge of
failure that the steel of
success is formed.

Hard Work Does Not
Guarantee Success, But
Success Does Not Happen
Without Hard Work.

- Dr. Jim Anderson

# Create Products Your Customers Want At A Price That They Are Willing To Pay!

Dr. Jim Anderson is available to provide training and coaching on the two topics that are the most important to product managers everywhere: how do I create the products that my customers want and what should I price them at?

Dr. Anderson believes that in order to both learn and remember what he says, product managers need to laugh. Each one of his speeches is full of fun and humor so that what he says "sticks" with everyone.

### Dr. Anderson's Product Management Training Includes:

1. How can you segment your market?
2. What problems are your customers having right now?
3. Which of your customer's problems does your product solve?
4. How much of this problem does your product solve?
5. How much will it cost your customer if they don't fix this problem?

Dr. Jim Anderson presents over 100 speeches per year. To invite Dr. Anderson to speak at your event, contact him at:

**Phone: 813-418-6970** or
**Email: jim@BlueElephantConsulting.com**

Blue Elephant Consulting
Speaking   Negotiating   Managing   Marketing

# Photo Credits:

Cover - Jayel Aheram
https://www.flickr.com/photos/aheram/

Chapter 1 - By: DRs Kulturarvsprojekt
https://www.flickr.com/photos/kulturarvsprojektet/

Chapter 2 - Philip Taylor
https://www.flickr.com/photos/9731367@N02/

Chapter 3 - Coryn Wolk
https://www.flickr.com/photos/backwards_dog/

Chapter 4 - Thomas Sun
https://www.flickr.com/photos/blogg3r/

Chapter 5 - Kevin O'Mara
https://www.flickr.com/photos/kevinomara/

Chapter 6 - Pelle Sten
https://www.flickr.com/photos/pellesten/

Chapter 7 - Amy the Nurse
https://www.flickr.com/photos/amyashcraft/

Chapter 8 - Lars Larsson
https://www.flickr.com/photos/friutbildning/

Chapter 9 - Jean-Jacques MARCHAND
https://www.flickr.com/photos/zenzak35/

Chapter 10 - K嘛
https://www.flickr.com/photos/kmar/

Chapter 11 - David Mulder
https://www.flickr.com/photos/113026679@N03/

Chapter 12 – Wikipedia
https://commons.wikimedia.org/wiki/File:Hadoop_logo.svg

# Other Books By The Author

**Product Management**

- Customer Lessons For Product Managers: Techniques For Product Managers To Better Understand What Their Customers Really Want

- Product Failure Lessons For Product Managers: Examples Of Products That Have Failed For Product Managers To Learn From

- Communication Skills For Product Managers: The Communication Skills That Product Managers Need To Know How To Use In Order To Have A Successful Product

- How To Have A Successful Product Manager Career: The Things That You Need To Be Doing TODAY In Order To Have A Successful Product Manager Career

- Product Manager Product Success: How to keep your product on track and make it become a success

## Public Speaking

- How To Rehearse In Order To Give The Perfect Speech: How to effectively rehearse your next speech to that your message be remembered forever!

- Secrets To Creating The Perfect Speech: How to create a speech that will make your message be remembered forever!

- Secrets To Organizing The Perfect Speech: How to organize the best speech of your life!

- Secrets To Planning The Perfect Speech

## CIO Skills

- How CIOs Can Make Innovation Happen: Tips And Techniques For CIOs To Use In Order To Make Innovation Happen In Their IT Department

- CIO Communication Skills Secrets: Tips And Techniques For CIOs To Use In Order To Become Better Communicators

- Managing Your CIO Career: Steps That CIOs Have To Take In Order To Have A Long And Successful Career

- CIO Business Skills: How CIOs can work effectively with the rest of the company!

## IT Manager Skills

- Secrets Of Effective Leadership For IT Managers: Tips And Techniques That IT Managers Can Use In Order To Develop Leadership Skills

- IT Manager Career Secrets: Tips And Techniques That IT Managers Can Use In Order To Have A Successful Career

- IT Manager Budgeting Skills: How IT Managers Can Request, Manage, Use, And Track Their Funding

## Negotiating

- Getting Ready To Win: How To Prepare For A Negotiation: What You Need To Do BEFORE A Negotiation Starts In Order To Get The Best Possible Deal

- Learn How To Argue In Your Next Negotiation: How To Develop The Skill Of Effective Arguing In A Negotiation In Order To Get The Best Possible Outcome

- How To Open Your Next Negotiation: How To Start A Negotiation In Order To Get The Best Possible Outcome

- Preparing For Your Next Negotiation: What You Need To Do BEFORE A Negotiation Starts In Order To Get The Best Possible Deal

**Miscellaneous**

- Power Distribution Unit (PDU) Secrets: What Everyone Who Works In A Data Center Needs To Know!

- Making The Jump: How To Land Your Dream Job When You Get Out Of College!

## What Product Managers Need To Know About World-Class Product Development

> This book has been written with one goal in mind – to show you how to make sure that the product that you need is the one that gets developed. We're going to show you how to work with your development team to get what you want.
>
> **Let's Make Your Product A Success!**

**What You'll Find Inside:**

- **HOW CAN PRODUCT MANAGERS PICK THE RIGHT TECHNOLOGY FOR OUR PRODUCTS?**

- **HOW YAHOO PRODUCT MANAGERS ARE KICKING GOOGLE'S BUTT**

- **FAST PRODUCT MANAGEMENT LESSONS FROM A PORSCHE 911**

- **WHAT EVERY PRODUCT MANAGER NEEDS TO KNOW ABOUT THE HADOOP DATABASE SOLUTION**

Dr. Jim Anderson brings his 4 college degrees coupled with over 25 years of real-world experience to this book. He's managed products at some of the world's largest firms as well as at start-ups. He's going to show you what you need to do in order to make your career a success!

www.ingramcontent.com/pod-product-compliance
Lightning Source LLC
Chambersburg PA
CBHW060413190526
45169CB00002B/875